Along the Way: Leadership Stories from Everyday Life

Stosh D. Walsh

Printed in the United States of America

First Printing: December 2012 by

2nd Place Press

Wheaton, IL

ISBN-13: 978-0615746777

ISBN-10: 0615746772

For Tammy, who saw first and believed first. Without her,
none of these stories are true.

Contents

Acknowledgements

Tammy, my love for you will never learn of ends. I am, in nearly every thing, an overachiever, most of which is because of you.

Ayla and Liam, your father loves you very much, and all that I have and am is yours. You are the gifts I have always wanted, and my pride in you will never fade.

Mom, you were my first hero, and will remain so forever.

Keith Powell (1934-2006), I stand on your shoulders, and always have. I know you would be proud, because you told me all the time. Your investment and generosity gave me the inestimable gift of possibility, and my life's fervent aim is to give it to others.

Solange and Niki, it wasn't easy, but here we are. I love you and your husbands and your children with all my strength, and all that lies within my power is yours but for the asking (and sometimes even when you don't).

Alex, thank you for making the choice to be Dad and Papa.

Scheri and Ken Bentsen, your steadfast example has informed these pages, and they are in your debt, as am I.

David Rendall, your persistent encouragement and belief have catalyzed this effort.

Elliott Anderson, my life's intersection with yours has shaped me in ways I am still uncovering. You have been, in turn, a father, brother, mentor and friend.

Susan Mosey, when I was in 4th grade, you invited me in to a world of academic achievement and discovery I did not know existed. This, in part, is the result.

Buck Webb, your editing prowess assists this work in telling ways. Pupils of your ability eclipse their teachers and become for them a source of pride.

All my former students, players, coaching clients and seminar attendees, you have helped me shape these thoughts and try their application. Thank you for your trust, and for your forgiveness as I made (and will make) mistakes along the way. I derive a great satisfaction from the privilege of being part of your leadership stories.

Finally, the One without whom nothing is possible—if every knee must bow, let mine be first.

Introduction

My first assignment in graduate school was to read a portion of one of Shakespeare's histories and write on the leadership insights I gleaned from it. I remember the settled feeling that came over me with the confirmation of a long held suspicion. Leadership lessons are everywhere: Shakespeare, movies, pop culture, sports, work, school and family.

Everyday encounters—rich in frustration, investment, humor, opportunity and reward—offer a refining crucible for our leadership. I spend a large portion of my work life as an executive coach, and though executive leadership is the domain of a select few, opportunities to lead at local levels are virtually endless regardless of title or position in life. Further, the consequences of leadership in those more everyday places are of no less import. In that sense, leadership is leadership. Although its applications differ, its values endure. Good leadership attributes and their corresponding behaviors are the same in every milieu.

I have had the privilege of interacting with leaders in dozens of Fortune 500 companies; I have read scores of leadership books; I have held leadership positions, and I have earned a graduate degree in leadership. All of these things have informed my knowledge and views of what leadership is and does, but none eclipse what I have gleaned about leadership from my everyday life, at home, with my wife and my two children. The lessons I have learned from my triumphs and mistakes at home have formed the basis not only for my own practice of leadership, but for my understanding of it and for my counsel to others on it also.

The following pages recount stories from everyday life in my family over a period of nearly 3 years. I have purposely kept them informal and arranged them somewhat randomly, as they are meant, for the most part, to stand alone. After each, I have fashioned questions I hope will provoke further consideration of how you might understand both your leadership and your everyday differently.

1 Initiative

I was out of town on business. While I was away, my wife made a passing remark about our lawn needing to be mowed. In response, my 8 year old son offered to mow it. So my wife started the lawnmower for him and set him loose.

Press pause. There's a good leadership lesson–let 'em try it! But I digress...

When I arrived home, I realized it had been done, but not by whom. I assumed that my wife had acquiesced to one of the 12 year old entrepreneurs who frequent our neighborhood with their advertisements for lawn care. Not long after I entered the house, I learned who had, in fact, done it.

I also learned what the expected rate for such service is.

"Between 4 and 6 bucks," my son reasoned.

Now, our lawn is reasonably sized, and would warrant significantly more than that from another service provider. In soliciting the views of some of my friends in passing, I received some wise counsel: let him feel like he has negotiated well. I asked him, "How much do you think it is worth?"

Again, "Between 4 and 6 bucks."

"How much would you charge someone else for that work?"

He thought for a moment, then responded, "10; 5 for the

front and 5 for the back."

"Deal," I agreed.

He felt like he'd negotiated well; he was proud of his effort and the money he'd earned.

I, however, was proud of his initiative.

Your Leadership Story

Whose initiative have you noticed lately?

How could you encourage or reward this initiative?

2 When to Get Out of the Way

My son and I were returning home from a long walk with our dog. A car headed toward us slowed, and finally stopped. Its driver leaned out of the open window and asked, "Do you know where Shady Lane is?"

"Hmm...," I thought aloud. "I know it's nearby, but I'm not sure where."

"Turn around; go back to Stoddard, and turn right. After that, it's the first street," interjected the voice of my not yet 8 year old son.

The driver looked at me, questioning.

"He's right," I remembered.

"Thank you," he looked at me, then corrected himself. "Thank you!" he said to my son before driving off.

"Good thing I remembered where Shady Lane is," my son said.

"Yeah, nice job," I replied.

My son doesn't know how to drive. We barely let him go a few blocks away on his bicycle. He's never had any training on reading a map, nor does he know anyone who lives on Shady Lane.

But that isn't the point. The point is that he knows where it is. He isn't supposed to know, and it doesn't matter how he knows, or how he remembered, just that he knows.

13

When that happens, a good leader has only one response: get out of the way and let the expert do the talking.

Your Leadership Story

To what extent are you willing to submit to the expertise of your followers?

What is your response when one of your followers knows more than you do? Celebration? Disappointment? Encouragement? Embarrassment?

3 First Things First

I rose early on Sunday and dressed for a run. I asked my daughter, who had also risen early, to walk the dog. She agreed, but as she was preparing to do so, I heard a whisper in my conscience: "Go with her."

I fought it at first–I wanted to start my run–but I found myself realizing that running, in this moment, would have been a selfish decision.

"If you wait just a second, I'll go with you," I said.

"OK," she smiled brightly.

It was simple; we went for a short walk with the dog, just up and down our street. We talked and laughed. The whole thing probably took 10 minutes.

When we came back inside, she proposed the idea to make breakfast for the rest of the family, who were still in bed.

"OK," I said. (When a 9 year old is eager to make her 7 year old brother breakfast in bed, you take it.)

We made breakfast together. She even took the coffee grinder to the outside porch to ensure its noise didn't awaken anyone. She wrote encouraging notes to put on the breakfast trays.

We delivered the breakfasts together and enjoyed the surprised and grateful responses. I encouraged her and thanked her for the great idea.

And *then* I went running–not as long as I'd planned to–but happier than I would have been otherwise.

Your Leadership Story

Who needs time with you? What personal interest might you need to delay or sacrifice on behalf of others?

What one thing in your life needs to be first, but currently isn't?

4 Doing Things Right Gets You...

~~Recognition~~ Ignored.

Unfortunately, most leaders tend to focus on what's wrong, or who's wrong, not on what's right, or who is doing the right things.

Yesterday I took my daughter to a local coffee establishment for a hot chocolate. I wanted to talk to her, and encourage her. You see, she is the kind of kid who does a lot of things right. She does her homework conscientiously, doesn't get in trouble at school, and tries to help other kids obey the rules.

But what she sees in her classroom, and sometimes in her home, makes her feel unappreciated. She often hears lectures about things that she didn't have anything to do with, and endures punishments designed for other kids but meted out on the entire class.

With this in mind, I said to her, "I know it's hard sometimes to do things right even when other people aren't. I really appreciate it, though, that you keep doing things right even though it's difficult, or even when other people keep getting attention for the wrong reasons."

True to form, she said, "Yeah, sometimes," but immediately started talking about something else. It just wasn't that big a deal to her. She does the right things because that's who she is.

As her Dad and as a leader, though, I have to make sure she knows I'm proud of her for that, and that I notice. A cup of hot chocolate and a few encouraging words are a small price to pay for assurance that she does.

Your Leadership Story

What percentage of your time do you spend with those who are doing things right compared to those who are getting into some trouble?

What message does this ratio send to those who are doing things right, and how can you reinforce it, or change it if necessary?

5 Who Are Your Followers?

Followership is an often overlooked, but essential, part of leadership.

Leaders gain the "right" to lead from only one source: their followers. Interestingly, though, too often we fail to identify who our followers are, or assume we have more, or fewer, than we actually do.

My son is learning this as he considers how to lead at school.

Today, we were talking about how his actions at school, whether positive or negative, influence others.

His take on followership was an interesting one: "Most of my followers are in a different classroom, so they don't notice what I'm doing."

He, like many other leaders, underestimates both the scope of his influence and the number of his followers. (Which, incidentally, is perhaps better than overestimating...)

My role in the situation was to invite him, and his leadership, into a larger world and into a greater understanding.

Not everyone who follows us is overt. Some people will view us as leaders and we will never know it. Others will know our names even though we do not know them.

My ongoing challenge to my son is the same as the challenge all leaders face: live like a leader all the time, not just when you are certain your "followers" are watching.

After my son and I had the talk about influencing people either positively or negatively, he expressed a frustration to me: "These 4 other boys in my class just keep following me!"

"That's a tremendous compliment to you," I said.

He was still frustrated. "If they like you and want to be around you," I continued, "then you have a great opportunity to lead them in a positive direction, just like we have discussed."

He nodded.

"I believe in you, and I think you can be a great example to these other boys. Your teacher told me that you are one of the positive leaders in your class, and I am very proud of you for that. If people are following you, make sure you are setting a great example for them. I know you can do it," I concluded.

They keep following... Having influence, being a leader, doesn't turn on and off, nor does it go away when we'd like a bit more privacy or a more convenient time. It is a curse in that we must be "always on," but it is also a significant blessing because it creates instant accountability; it keeps us humble when we fail; it forces us to examine ourselves and apologize when necessary (often publicly); and, perhaps most of all, invites intentionality.

They keep following... Where will we take them?

Your Leadership Story

How can you be more aware of who chooses to follow you?

Do you have a clear direction and intent for your followers?

6 Where Are We Taking Them?

My daughter sings with a children's choir at our church. Yesterday, they had a Christmas party. Kindly, she asked the choir director if her brother could attend the party, although he does not participate in choir. The director agreed, so both of my children attended the party last night.

This morning as we were talking about it over breakfast, it surfaced that my son had played the fool's part on a few occasions and was doing things to amuse other children that were distracting them from the evening's program. Obviously, this was a concern, so I asked him a few questions about it, starting with, "Is this true?"

"Well, kind of," he answered sheepishly.

"Yes, or no?" I pressed.

"Probably."

"Yes, or no?" again, I pressed the issue.

"Yes," he replied.

"So what do you think you should do about that?" I inquired.

"Not do it again."

"Anything else?"

"Apologize."

We'd agreed on what was to be done, and a few minutes

later I spoke to him privately and encouraged his leadership. I told him that since he is a leader, what he does matters. People will follow him whether he demonstrates positive or negative behavior, and so it is even more important for him to provide a positive example now that he is more aware of others following him.

Your Leadership Story

How do you measure the impact of your leadership?

How do you handle it when you must apologize as a leader?

7 They Know What They WANT. Do You Know What They NEED?

"What would you like for breakfast?" I asked my son.

"Crunch Berries," he replied.

"Not unless you are having something else with it," I said.

"But that's all I want," came the predictable retort.

He knows exactly what he wants. But it is my job to know what he needs.

Though it made me unpopular this morning, Crunch Berries weren't on the menu; a banana was.

The point, of course, isn't to turn my 7 year old son into an ascetic. The point is to enable him to make good decisions when he is older, decisions based on need, not want. Helping him to do that is worth risking his displeasure or argument. It's worth leading him instead of acquiescing.

And it creates reserves, both for me as a leader, and for his expectations, when his future wants (movies, video games, TV, dessert) conflict with his needs, which is sure to happen.

Probably tomorrow.

Your Leadership Story

Do you know what your followers need?

Are you willing to take unpopular stands and risk their anger when they don't get what they want?

8 "Are You Proud of It?"

My son is neither very neat nor very organized. This is not a big deal, and we work around it most of the time.

Today, however, he was "cleaning his room" by taking things that were on the floor and putting them on surfaces throughout his room–his bottom bunk, his dresser, his desk... In essence, his version of "clean" was "off the floor."

His less than thorough approach to cleaning his room presented me with a leadership opportunity. When I called him back to his room to do the rest of the cleaning, I made sure that the first thing I said to him was, "Thank you for being willing to clean your room and not complaining about it." Next, I told him that I appreciated what he had done, and that I trusted him to do a thorough job. I told him that I wasn't going to check his room again, because I was sure he'd do exactly what he knew was a complete cleaning now that he knew what was expected.

When he finished a few minutes later, he called me to come and look. "I trust you," I told him. "Are you proud of your effort?"

"Yes," he responded.

"Then you are finished," I said without looking into his room.

I was trusting both his effort and his standards after I'd thanked him and encouraged him. Was the room as clean as it would have been had I done it? Probably not. Was it more clean than it would have been had I not trusted him to make the decision himself based on knowing that I thought he could do it and wasn't going to check up on him? Definitely.

Next time, I might not have to say anything at all.

Your Leadership Story

Where must expectations between you and your followers be clearer?

How can you cultivate a sense of ownership and pride in others with whom you partner?

9 I'm Proud of Your Failure?!?

We were down by a goal in the waning moments of our last soccer game. My son, who is one of the youngest players on the team (and therefore one of the least developed skill-wise) was playing forward.

He took up an intelligent position in the center of the penalty area, just as we'd been working on in practice.

Then it happened.

The perfect cross.

One of his teammates sent a terrific ball right into his path, and he was alone in front of the goal. It was exactly as we'd been rehearsing in the weeks leading up to the game. Now all he had to do was kick it in, and we'd be tied.

The ball arrived, right at his feet.

He swung his leg back…

…and missed. Whiffed. No contact with the ball, and the moment was lost.

We lost the game 3-2.

Afterward, I called him over, picked him up to give him a big hug, and told him, "I'm proud of you; do you know why?"

"Why?" he said, still a little disappointed.

"Because you did exactly what we practiced," I said. "You went to the exact right spot for the cross, and you tried to kick it in with your first touch instead of controlling it, which is the right thing to do. And I'd rather have you do the right thing, and have the right idea, even if you miss, than to see you score but develop habits that you'll have to change later."

He wasn't totally convinced, but it made him feel a bit better.

I was being completely honest with him, both as a coach, and as his dad. I was very proud of him. He'll score a lot of goals later because he's doing things the right way–trying to do what is difficult instead of doing it the easy way and then not being able to do it at a more advanced level later. It won't be long before his coordination and skill level catch up to what his mind is trying to do, and when that happens, he'll score every time that cross is played to him.

I'll be proud of him then, too.

Your Leadership Story

What are you doing to encourage people who follow you to try difficult things? Even to fail?

How can you encourage followers to avoid the easy way in favor of long term successful habits?

10 You Get What You...

How would you finish that sentence?

Most people say, "pay for."

As leaders, we need to think about it differently. "You get what you measure," is a good start, but that can lead to transactional leadership, which, while sometimes appropriate, doesn't usually result in meaningful change.

Today, I am reminded that as leaders, we get what we encourage. That is, we get what we invest in. This, wielded well, means we get what we expect.

Pause with me for a minute. If we get what we expect as leaders, we are, in some way, able to predict the future, to know in advance what will transpire because of our actions, which can be very powerful indeed.

I read regularly with my son. We read aloud. He reads a page, then I read a page, and so on. Two days ago, I encouraged him because he pronounced the word "inquisitive" perfectly, and, when asked, knew exactly what it meant.

I returned home today and he greeted me with, "Dad, today I read the word 'unauthorized.'"

"Do you know what that means?" I asked.

"It means when you don't have permission," he responded, "but I don't know what 'authorized' means."

"Well, if 'unauthorized' means you don't have permission,

what do you think?"

"It must mean when you do have permission," he concluded.

He wants to learn; moreover, he wants to demonstrate what he has learned. In part, this is because we have invested in this together, and I have encouraged it over time.

And, incidentally, I'm getting exactly what I expected, and I couldn't be happier.

Your Leadership Story

What do you encourage, invest in and expect?

How have you fostered independence and a desire to learn in your associates?

11 'Have to' and 'Want to'

My children are old enough to perform certain tasks, and assist with the keeping of our household. One task is walking the dog. Both my daughter and my son do this faithfully most of the time, but on occasion, complaining accompanies cooperation.

Given this background, something ironic has been happening lately. Every time I walk the dog, my daughter creeps out the door a minute or two after I have gone, and tries to sneak up on me. Sometimes she is successful; other times I see her coming. In either case, though, we end up finishing the walk together, talking and holding hands.

She doesn't always like to walk the dog on her own, but most of the time when I walk the dog, she wants to join me.

What's the difference?

"Have to" versus "Want to."

She follows me because she wants to, because she likes being outside, and because she likes our dog. (It probably helps that I pick up his mess when we're together also...)

What do your followers "want to" do? What do they "have to" do? More importantly, how can you help them do more of the "want to" even in the midst of the "have to?" What would that take?

Important caveat: we're not talking about getting people to do things they don't want to do because we, their leaders, want them to do it. There's a definition of leadership out there that goes something like: "leadership is getting people to do things they didn't want to do, and making them feel like they want to do it." This is a total myth. Leadership is not about persuading, or worse, manipulating, people to do things they didn't want to do. It is, however, about finding out what they do, in fact, want to do, and helping them to do more of that. It is also about helping them to see connections between what they "have to" do, and what they "want to" do, so that the "have tos" become more bearable.

So maybe the better question is, "What do your followers 'want to' do?"

Your Leadership Story

Do you know what motivates each individual on your team?

What steps are you taking to align their motivations and talents to what needs done?

12 "We Could Do This Every Week or Something."

My son and I were playing with Nerf guns–shooting foam darts at a target he'd made. When that lost its appeal, we started to invent games: see who could hit the doorknob first; turn out the lights and shine a flashlight on the wall, then shoot the light; see how many darts we could get to stick to the wall; shoot darts sticking on the wall and try to knock them down...

We stood up and shot; we lay down and shot; we shared darts; we competed with each other and against each other.

Then, tentatively, my son said, "We could do this every week or something."

He didn't want it to end.

"Yeah," I said. (I was having fun too.)

It takes me by surprise sometimes, how much he wants to be with me. It hardly matters what we do; he just wants to be where I am, do what I'm doing, watch how I act, and have my approval.

That it takes me by surprise betrays how much time I spend thinking about it. But he thinks about it often; much more than I do. It isn't that I don't look forward to spending time with him, but that I am taking for granted, even overlooking, what happens during that time.

It is that time that develops attributes in my son, and shapes how he thinks I perceive him.

Your Leadership Story

As leaders, what attributes are you developing in others?

How do they think you perceive them? How do you know?

13 When Fishing Isn't About Catching Fish

My son wanted to go fishing. We'd postponed it a day, but today was the day. He could barely wait, but several things had to be done first. I had work to do and so did the rest of the family.

By late afternoon, we were on our way. The first thing I said to him was, "I'm sorry it took so long, but I'm glad we're going."

"That's OK," he replied cheerfully.

We talked as we walked to the pier.

"You can fish too if you want," he said, offering to sacrifice his own enjoyment for mine, as we have only one rod–a Batman-themed kid's rod.

"I'll help you cast if you want, but I'll probably just watch and talk to you," I offered.

We arrived at the pier and I prepared the bait (a lump of wheat bread formed into a ball). After several failed attempts, we tried a new strategy: simply lowering the hook and bobber into the water where we could see it, and trying to get the small bluegill to bite.

It worked! Not more than 5 minutes after employing our new strategy, my son had caught a fish about the size of my hand. I removed the hook and released the fish. "Let's try to catch another," I said.

"I doubt we will," came the reply.

"Don't doubt yourself–you just caught one, and I'm sure you can do it again!" I encouraged. "Always believe in yourself; I believe in you," I told him.

"Do you have your phone?" he asked.

"Yes, why?"

"Can I call Mom and tell her we caught a fish?"

"Sure," I smiled.

He made the call, and left a message when Mom didn't answer. I prepared the line for another attempt, and we tried to lower the bait a little further, thinking there might be some larger fish deeper in the water.

We were right. Not long after, we watched our bobber disappear, and my son yelled, "Reel it in, Dad!"

I couldn't. The fish was too large for the meager strength of the rod we were using. I had to grab the line and pull it in hand over hand. It was a 14″ bass, probably about 4 pounds. We were both quite surprised.

I released the fish, at the cost of cutting the line, which meant our fishing trip was over.

"That's OK," my son said. "I've caught 3 fish in my life now, and that last one we caught was the biggest of all! I've never seen a fish that big so close! And I helped you catch it by telling you when to reel it in."

"That's right," I said, more than willing to share the credit for the catch.

Next time, he will believe in himself even more.

Your Leadership Story

How do you encourage self-belief in your constituency?

How do you share credit and recognize accomplishment among your team?

14 Motive

"Let's run; c'mon!" my daughter said, breaking into a stride through the parking lot.

I pressed the remote button to open the van door for her as I walked quickly through the rain.

She reached the car well ahead of me, and began to climb into the front seat.

"Don't!" I said in vain as she put her wet foot on my seat.

She was only trying to reciprocate–trying to open the door for me so that I wouldn't get wet; just like I had done for her.

I was more concerned, though, about her getting in the front seat, and subsequently about my seat getting wet, than I was about her motive.

Unfortunately, her great motive was trumped by my bad assumption, and by my greater concern for what was happening than for what she was trying to do.

Suspend judgment; discern motive.

I made a mental note of that today–next time I'll react less to what is happening and more to motive.

Your Leadership Story

What checks and balances do you employ to suspend judgment and discern others' motives?

As a leader, do you typically assume the best or the worst?

15 Permission vs. Trust

I borrowed a friend's car today.

Doing so reminded me of an essential ingredient of leadership: trust.

Obviously, I have enough trust capital with my friend that he was willing to lend me his car–that's the obvious point–but there's more: I picked up his car from his house when he wasn't home. He left the car parked in his driveway with his entire set of keys in the ignition and told me to come by and pick it up the night before.

Two extrapolations of trust merit mentioning here: first, he was, in essence, whether he'd thought about it or not, trusting me not just with his car, but with his home and anything else that I might have been able to get into with those keys. Second, he trusted his community, and his neighbors, by leaving the car unattended with the keys in the ignition.

So what are the ingredients of trust? Is it knowing that the trusted party will not do anything unbecoming, and assuming the best in people until they prove us wrong?

I submit that it can be these things, but that in order for trust to be actionable–the basis of a relationship between a leader and follower–it must be based on two things: faith and shared expectations.

My friend loaned me his car because he had faith not that nothing would happen to his car while I had it, but in my ability to ensure that nothing would happen. He trusted me because he believed that his expectation of how to care for his car and my expectation were similar, if not exactly the same. But it was trust because he did not clarify that with me up front.

It is possible to give permission, but not trust.

Your followers know the difference.

Your Leadership Story

Do you trust your followers, or do they just have your permission?

Who merits more trust than you are currently extending?

16 The Value of Remembering

My son was invited to play at a friend's house just a few blocks away, and my daughter's plan was to watch a movie while he was gone.

But I remembered something.

She'd wanted to go for a bike ride "with you guys [her parents]." (Often my kids ride their bikes while my wife and I run.)

"We'll ride our bikes to his friend's house," I said. "Would you like to ride around for a little while afterward?"

Her smile gave me my answer.

So we did. After we dropped my son off at his friend's, we raced; we took a "secret path," and came home a way we'd never travelled before.

…and we still watched a movie when we got home.

Remember what your followers want and need–the rewards can be tremendous.

Your Leadership Story

Who in your life needs to come "along for the ride?"

When was the last time you did something fun with one of your people, just because it was what they wanted to do?

17 Motivation vs. Inspiration

One of the things we've been talking about a lot lately at our house is the motivation behind why we do things.

My wife and I use various means of positive reinforcement to lead our children. This, however, is not without its drawbacks. The main one is that our children have started to expect some kind of reward each time they demonstrate kindness, complete a chore, or do something without being asked.

These things, of course, are mostly common courtesies, which is why we, and just about everyone else, want to teach them to our children.

But what about the reward? What shall we say about that?

"_____ is its own reward." You've no doubt heard that, and while it might be true, it is, or has become, cliché to the point of lacking meaning.

No, it is not about the reward; it is about the heart, the intrinsic motivation.

I have come to believe that leaders cannot motivate others. We can inspire, but people motivate themselves. I heard a speaker say that once, and wrestled with it for a long time, but after that process I believe it to be true.

Inspiration, then, must be our goal. For inspiration is not as transient as motivation can be. If I reinforce the positive behavior of my children with a tangible reward, they are motivated, but only for a time. This is not wrong in itself, but to see that behavior perpetuated without the reward, in order for that motivation to become intrinsic for my followers, I must inspire them.

They must be inspired, and not motivated, because there will come a time when doing the right thing, the considerate thing, the ethical thing will mean foregoing external reward, not reaping it.

And that is the moment when my leadership in their lives will be measured.

If I have inspired them, they will be motivated to evaluate with their own compasses what the best paths for their journeys are, and they will continue to choose those best paths long after I am no longer the main voice of influence in their lives.

If I am successful as a leader, their motivation will be to live well, and no reward will be able to alter that.

Your Leadership Story

As a leader, how can you make the shift from motivating others to inspiring them?

What kinds of behaviors do you want your followers to demonstrate without reward or fear of consequence?

18 There's a Frog in Our Tent!

My family and I went camping last weekend. Overall, it was a fun time, with one exception: on the first night, it rained–a lot.

Water began to make its way inside the tent, and my wife and I shifted things around to minimize the damage and discomfort. My son slept through the storms, but my daughter awakened almost immediately.

The three of us tried, with varying degrees of success, to return to sleep. Just as I was reaching that coveted destination, I heard my daughter's frenzied voice say, "There's a frog in our tent!"

I tried, in vain, to assure her that though she could hear the sounds of frogs and rain outside, it was impossible that a frog had entered our tent. She insisted, and so we changed the orientation of her sleeping bag so that her head was on the opposite side of where she thought she'd seen the frog.

I tucked her back in, and then, peeking out from over the edge of her covering, she said, "I'd feel better if you held my hand."

I was tired, damp, and frustrated. I knew that trying to hold my daughter's hand and sleep at the same time would be next to impossible. The truth was, I didn't really want to hold her hand in that moment.

But I did.

"OK," I smiled at her.

She wriggled her fingertips out of the top of the sleeping bag and I reached over to grab them.

An hour or two later, just after sunrise, I awakened to her shaking my shoulder.

"Look! See, I told you!"

There, just as she indicated, was the clear silhouette of a small frog that had jumped on to the outside of our tent.

I acknowledged it, and we both went back to sleep for a little while.

When we'd all awakened, she leaned across my back and said, "You sure did make me feel better last night."

Mission accomplished.

We all have moments when we do something that we don't really want to do because it will help someone else. As a leader, I find that the more often I subjugate my own interests for those of others, the better I lead.

Your Leadership Story

When one of your constituents needs your help, encouragement or intervention, what is your typical first reaction?

What sacrifices do you regularly make on behalf of those who follow you?

19 Because of Who You Are

I experienced 2 incidents this week that reinforced the notion that we are ever in the spotlight as leaders, whether we intend to be or not. I would have taken both of these incidents for granted but for being attuned to opportunities to wield the influence others grant me.

The first occurred as I was shaving. My son came in to the bathroom and immediately wanted to shave also. This in itself was not a surprise, as he does this from time to time, but then he asked me a good question, "Dad, why do you shave?"

"Because I have to," I responded.

"Do I need to shave?" he asked.

"Well, not really," I said. "Not yet."

"Is it fun to shave?" he continued.

"Not really."

"Is it fun for you to shave?" I asked.

"No, not really," he replied.

"Then why do you do it?"

"I guess because you do."

I guess because you do. That won't be the only thing he does just because I do it, and I am certain that whoever your followers are, there are things they are doing, or trying to do, for one simple reason: because the leader does it.

The next incident involved not one of my own children, but one of their teammates on the soccer team I coach. We saw him at the 4th of July parade in our town and greeted him. As he walked away, he moved quickly to his mom, and I overheard his raised voice telling her that he had seen "his coach," a fact about which he was obviously animated.

I hadn't done anything special or out of the ordinary. I was just "his coach."

I was just shaving–something I do without thinking about it.

But someone else is thinking about it. Someone else is watching.

Live up to their eyes.

Edit: I've since grown a beard, so no more shaving. Guess who wants to grow one too?

Your Leadership Story

How can you cultivate your awareness that others are watching?

How can you instill this ethic in those you influence?

49

20 When Followers Are Away

My children are staying with close family friends for a few days to attend a camp.

In some ways, this provides a welcome respite from the norm, and enables my wife and I to spend time together without the usual interruptions and distractions of our regular routine.

It is also, however, disconcerting for a few reasons. First, the obvious concerns about how our children will behave in our absence linger. This, though, provides an insight into leadership: it is how followers conduct themselves when the leader is not present that reflects most accurately the quality of the leader's influence and training. Followers must be trusted to carry themselves well, praised when they do, and gently restored when they do not. Otherwise, they will remain in constant need of their leaders' actual presence, which hinders growth and desirable outcomes of all kinds.

Maybe more important, though, is the second reason: it is disconcerting for me as a leader, and I must be aware of my own feelings in order to lead well. The simple fact is that I miss my kids. I am affected when they are away; I am emotionally attached to them because of my compassion for them, my investment in them, and my hope for their futures.

And this is a good gauge for how committed we are as leaders. How emotionally attached are we to those who follow us? How invested are we in hoping for the futures of those who look to us for leadership?

We can find out by listening to our hearts when they are away.

Your Leadership Story

How do you express care for your followers?

How might you customize your approach to each, demonstrating care for them in the way they receive it best?

21 Pride Comes Before...

"Pride comes before a fall."

But not if your pride is in others.

I've learned something very important about leadership in the last few weeks, as each member of my family has accomplished something that stirred my pride in them.

First, I'd been coaching my son in soccer, and we'd come to the final game. He'd started out sheepish, not being very aggressive, discouraged when his team wasn't winning, and not very willing to give his best effort. During this last game, though, something changed. We'd been playing in the yard, working on skills, and I'd seen him improve just because he'd been gaining familiarity with the ball, but this was different. All of a sudden he had confidence.

During the previous several games, he hadn't yet scored a goal, and I knew he wanted badly to do so. Not long into the final game, his moment came. The ball came out of the group to him, and he kicked it through the maze of legs to find the net for our team's first goal. He celebrated by running and sliding on the ground (I think his parents let him watch too much professional soccer on television), obviously pleased with his first tally. Late in the game, though, the teams were tied, and he got the ball on the sideline. I barely had a moment to wonder what decision he would make before he made it: he took one player on, cutting to the inside, then another, freeing himself for an unobstructed shot–another goal! The winning goal!

I smiled, and blinked back tears as I realized that I was

prouder of my son's goal than I had ever been of one of my own, or of anyone else's, though I played and coached at a high level. In a father's eyes, this might as well have been the goal that sealed the World Cup.

A few days later, I was informed by my daughter's school that she would be receiving a special award at the end of the year ceremony at her school. I rearranged my schedule to be there, and learned that a piece of art she had produced–a cardinal on an evergreen branch– had been chosen to grace the front of the holiday greeting card for the next school year. As a result, the school had it framed, and plans to display it in a prominent place.

But the great thing was that they hadn't told my daughter. For her, it was a complete surprise. She heard her name called, and came to the front, where the principal and her art teacher met her with the framed artwork for her to display to the rest of the school. She was proud and embarrassed all at once, and again, I blinked back the tears of pride, knowing that I was more pleased with this recognition than I ever had been of those I have received myself. Already she has two framed pictures on display at her school, though she has been there only a year.

And then, last Saturday, I rose early to run a 5k race with my wife–her first–and encourage her through it. I kept time for her and tried to help her maintain the pace at which she'd trained, adding encouragement from time to time. As she increased the pace for the last stretch of the race, I was proud of how well she finished, and of the dedication she'd shown in getting to the point of being able to run that far. A few hours after the race, we looked at the posted results, and learned that she'd finished in the top quarter of her age group in her very first race! And one last time I felt more proud of what another had done than of what I had accomplished myself.

Initially, I think it is possible only in our closest relationships that we are happier for the accomplishment of others than we are of our own, yet it is the maturation of leadership that extends this pride to others who are outside that immediate circle, and draws them into it as a result.

Pride comes before a fall, but not when you are leading well.

Your Leadership Story

Of whom are you proud? Do they know the extent of your pride? How could you demonstrate it more readily?

What are you doing intentionally to increase the circle of those in whom you have pride?

22 Accommodating the Needs of Others

My wife handles the hair braiding duties in our house. (This should come as a surprise to no one.)

She was away tonight, though, so I bathed our kids and got them ready for bed. I do this regularly, and I actually can braid my daughter's hair, but it is never as good as when my wife does it. Furthermore, my wife often uses a French braid, which is better, as it stays in overnight despite having been slept on.

I've watched her do this many times, and decided that tonight I would try it. Most of the reason for this is that I know my daughter likes it better when she has a "tight braid," as she calls it.

It turned out OK. Still not as good as my wife's, but when it was finished, my daughter turned around and said, "This one is better than your usual braids."

Mission accomplished.

Simple and mundane, but meaningful because it sent the message to my daughter that I was willing not only to try something I might not be good at for her, but also to learn her preferences and seek to accommodate them.

Your Leadership Story

Who would benefit from accommodation from you?

Whose preferences should you learn to lead them better?

23 Intentionality--When Everyone Is Looking

My son and I were sitting in the car, just talking and enjoying the shelter we had from the brutal cold outside. We were waiting for my wife, who had gone inside the school to pick up my daughter. A woman came out first; I spied her in my rearview mirror. She came to her car, which we'd parked next to, and began to scrape the ice from its windows. She was struggling, and hadn't turned her car on first to utilize the defroster–a big mistake.

"Wait here," I told my son. "I'm going to help her, and I'll be right back."

I hopped out and finished clearing her windows while she started her car. The entire episode only took a moment, and when I came back around to open the door upon returning to my vehicle, my son peered through the window, greeting me with the "thumbs up" sign.

I opened the door.

"Good choice, Dad," he said. "We've been learning at TruthWorks (a church program) about good choices, and that was a good choice."

It was a simple thing to do, of course, and didn't require much of my time or effort. By itself, it is not a memorable event. In terms of leadership, though, it is consequential because while it was a good deed endeavored, it was also a leadership opportunity missed.

My son was watching–how could he not have been? Yet I didn't think of it until after the moment had passed. How much better could that moment have been if I had taken just a few seconds to explain why it was important for me to get out of the car and help, or, better yet, given him the option of coming with me? Sure, he got something valuable out of watching his dad do something for someone else, but too often we let others watch while we perform, and that is not the goal.

So it is with leadership. We absolutely must be intentional not just about doing things, but, perhaps more importantly, about seeing things in a way that would enable us to pass leadership lessons and experiences on to others. Call it mentoring, development, or something else, but we must see every moment, however small, as an opportunity to lead, and to give someone else a chance to lead with us.

It is likely that my son will remember what he saw, and I am happy for that. Next time, though, I will ensure he repeats it, because it will be his experience also.

Your Leadership Story

Which occurs more often: your followers joining you, or your followers watching you perform?

As a leader, to what degree have you cultivated the habit of mentoring through every day moments?

24 Negative Examples

I've heard it many times in conversations, during seminars I've facilitated, or from people I've coached: "I learned what *not* to do..."

I've had a major realization in the last week or two: negative examples give us something to run away from, but they do not provide a direction, which is perhaps the most important aspect of leadership, whether you are leading yourself or others.

My stark realization of the last two weeks is that I have spent my whole life running from a negative example.

My father succumbed to drug addiction and suicide when I was very young. I have certainly been intentional to avoid his mistakes, but it has been reactive. I have responded to the circumstance. Now, I realize more fully that it is direction, not just intentionality, that I require.

The question I asked myself yesterday was, "How far must you run away from something in order to escape it?" I outran my past long ago, but I kept running. I had intent, but no direction, a vision for others, but not for myself. I have allowed the difference in my circumstances, and the difference I would make for others, to define me (a reactive approach), instead of allowing those things to be byproducts of the who and what I am becoming (a directional approach).

It illustrates the difference between, "I will *never* be...," and "I will be..."

One is reactive, the other directional; one yields distance, the other possibilities.

To possibilities, then.

Your Leadership Story

Are your life and leadership characterized primarily by moving toward, or away, from something?

How do you determine what to move toward?

25 A Good Heart

I came home from a business trip last night, and while I was eating a late dinner, my children were watching *The Hunchback of Notre Dame*.

Not far into the movie, Quasimodo is crowned "king of fools" and people begin to throw things at him, tying him down and ridiculing him.

Upon seeing this, my daughter began to cry aloud.

I turned off the video and moved to sit next to her and give her a hug.

"You have a good heart, Sweetie," I told her.

That, for me, is an essential attribute of a good leader.

Your Leadership Story

How can you demonstrate empathy to those who follow you, especially when their talents are different from yours?

How can you invite more empathy into your circle of trusted others?

26 Keeping Your Word

"But I didn't shake hands or anything," my son protested.

He'd made a deal with his sister. It was a silly deal: he'd wear camouflage pants to match hers if she brought him a shirt from the laundry downstairs. But now he was dressed in different pants at breakfast, upsetting his sister, and I'd told him to change clothes.

When he came back down, I asked him why he thought he had to do that, but he was too embarrassed to say, so I asked him if he wanted me to tell him why I thought it was important. He said yes, and I explained that keeping his word and not making excuses about it, even when the matter seems unimportant, reveals our character.

And our leadership.

Your Leadership Story

Do you keep your promises absolutely, even small ones?

How well would others say you keep your promises? How could you find out?

27 Partnership

This morning, my children tried to surprise my wife and I with breakfast in bed. But I ruined it for them by getting up too early. Knowing my wife was awake also, the surprise might have been doomed to failure, but a partnership salvaged it.

The three of us worked together quickly to keep the surprise intact for my wife. My son came up with the idea, I executed the plan, and my daughter delivered the product. Initially, they were both disappointed, because they wanted to be the ones who did it all, but I think they realized that without the partnership, the breakfast might not have come off.

I told my daughter, "Sometimes we have to partner with other people because they can help us do something better or faster, or maybe they are more able to do something than we are. Without the idea, though, and without someone who can deliver it, nothing happens, so we have a good partnership."

Have a clear result in mind, figure out who is best suited to the roles required, agree to partner, and deliver!

We did it at my house this morning. The breakfast was simple, nothing memorable.

But the shared leadership of partnering is.

Your Leadership Story

Where are you partnering as a leader?

Where should you be partnering, but aren't?

28 Trying Something New

This weekend, I took my kids into the city to spend a day.

One of the places we visited was Navy Pier, where a large Ferris wheel provides a panoramic view of the Chicago skyline to the West, and Lake Michigan to the East. The Ferris wheel makes one full revolution in 6-7 minutes before passengers exit the ride.

My daughter was ecstatic–she couldn't wait to get on. My son was scared, and started to dig in for a fight.

Trying something new requires courage, and sometimes encouragement. This is a fine line to walk as a leader, though, because we must not manipulate, or even appear to manipulate our followers into doing something.

I was just about to scrap the idea, when I asked my son a question: "If I gave you a reward, would you ride the Ferris wheel?"

When he smiled and said, "Yes!" I knew that he'd been playing it up, and wasn't quite as scared as he was portraying, especially as his tendency is toward the dramatic from time to time.

So we went.

But when we got on, he was scared anyway, and didn't want to look outside our carriage.

This moment, not the time spent persuading him to board the carriage, provided the leadership opportunity.

I could easily have told him to "gut it out"–after all, the ride only lasted 6 or 7 minutes. Instead, though, I let my daughter enjoy the ride, and allowed my son to hide his face in my arm. He dared to peek out from the safety of my side every few seconds, gathering real bravery only after I told him (truthfully) that the ride was more than half over, and that we were on our way down.

As I thought about it more, I concluded that although he was afraid, allowing him to feel that emotion and to experience the fear gives him permission not just to be afraid, but to dare to try something new in the future with less anxiety. It also increases his trust in me. He did, after all, survive, and even told my wife later about how he'd seen Lake Michigan.

Conquering fear by trying something new is not a one time proposition. It is something that often takes time and multiple experiences, and it is a leader's responsibility to create an environment in which that is possible.

Your Leadership Story

How are you lending courage to others?

How are you creating a safe place for others, one in which they can admit when they are scared and receive support?

29 The Best at...

My bias as a leader is to focus on what I (and others) do well, as opposed to making remediation attempts. This extends to my family, where I am always trying to emphasize what my wife and children do at a level of excellence.

I have evidence this week that this approach is beginning to bear fruit.

My daughter, who is a talented artist, decided to use her gifts to make me a certificate. It said, "This certificate is for Dad, for being the best at RISK (a strategy board game I enjoy playing)." Her next effort was for my wife, who received a certificate for being the best chef in the world. Her brother was recognized for being the best at video games. I saw also a few certificates in progress for her friends at school.

My daughter is 8 1/2 years old. Already she understands an aspect of human nature, and leadership, that many well-seasoned leaders never master: it's about people.

Obviously, many other facets of leadership exist, but few are as important as recognizing that which others do well and eliciting the best from them.

Lead on, my dear.

Your Leadership Story

To what extent do you strive to see the best in others?

How have you recognized the best in them?

30 Be Willing

I was traveling for work, and the session I was leading did not begin until the afternoon, so I had the morning to myself. My hotel was a very short walk from the beach, and so I decided to rise early, watch the sunrise, and then go for a run.

I learned something about leadership in those morning hours.

We've all heard the expression, "the early bird gets the worm." An element of leadership truth resides in that statement. It is not so much about being first or best, though those things are often important. Rather, it is the willingness to do things that others will not do in order to reap the rewards of having done so.

I rose earlier than normal because I know that watching the sun rise over the ocean is something I will only rarely have the chance to do. The same holds true for running on the beach, and, for that matter, swimming in it, which I did right after my run.

Often as leaders, it is the willingness to try something new, lose a little sleep, or endure some discomfort that yields the reward of impact, satisfaction or victory.

I realized later that while I might take doing something like this for granted, not everyone does. When I checked out of the hotel, the concierge asked me, "How was your stay?"

"Great," I replied.

"What did you do?" he asked.

"Watched the sun rise, went for a run, swam..."

"In the pool, right?" he said, seeking to clarify.

"No, in the ocean," I said.

"I'd like to shake your hand," he said, extending his.

For me, it wasn't cold; it wasn't winter. Most of that, of course, is climate. I am from Chicago, and it was nearly 70 degrees warmer in Miami Beach than it was at home.

But it drove home the point for me: not everyone does this, nor would they want to.

As leaders, if we're willing to do something a little out of the ordinary, good things can happen. That is very satisfying all by itself, but more important than that, it is inspiring to others, it creates possibilities, asks "Why not?" instead of "Why?"

And "Why not?" is a question only the willing can answer.

Your Leadership Story

When have you done something that others weren't willing to do?

How did it make you feel, and what was the result?

31 I Wouldn't Ask My People to Do Anything I Couldn't Do

Last night we made pizza. When I was a teenager, I worked in a few pizzerias, so it is always my job whenever we have pizza night to shape the crust and make the pies.

While I was in the process of doing this, my daughter asked if she could help me. I consented, and began to show her how to hold her hands and press the dough so that it would form crust, then use a fork to make holes in the flat surface so that it doesn't rise and ruin the pizza.

I could teach her because I knew how to do it; I've acquired the skill.

It also made me think of leadership. I think one of the biggest myths about leadership is the notion that leaders cannot, or should not, expect followers to do something that the leader can not do herself.

This is a mistake. It is true of teaching, but not true of leadership. Leadership is having the relationship to influence others. Often this involves soliciting the talents and skills of those who have something greater to contribute than the leader does.

In my coaching days, nearly every player on my roster was more skilled than I had been in my prime (and good thing, or we might never have won a game), but that certainly did not preclude me from leading them.

It helps, of course, to have a modicum of skill or aptitude for the matter at hand, but it is not a prerequisite.

Leadership is more than that.

Your Leadership Story

As a leader, do you surround yourself with experts whose talent or knowledge exceeds yours?

Do you welcome the notion that those currently following you could one day be in positions of greater authority or visibility than yours?

32 You Have to Accept...

I returned from a business trip last night, and was enjoying breakfast with my children this morning. My son was eager to give me a gift he had made at school, and though it is a week before Christmas, I relented, much to the chagrin of my daughter.

She said to me, "Don't you want to wait until Christmas to open your presents, and not open them early?"

"It's OK," I replied. "Your brother is eager to give this gift, and so it is fine with me to open it now."

She just frowned.

I reached over and brushed her pretty hair away from her face, and said, "Did you know that when I was younger, I never wanted to open my presents early either? Even when other people did, I still waited until Christmas, so you and I are alike."

"But now you have to accept..." she began.

"What kids want," I smiled as I finished her sentence.

I accommodate; I adjust. It is, in the end, not very consequential whether or not a gift is opened early. However, it is consequential to my children at this stage in their lives, and so it becomes consequential to my leadership that I "accept" without becoming rigid or doing things only in the ways that I prefer them.

Sometimes, leaders have to adjust.

In bigger situations, this is about agility vs. non-negotiables. We can't adjust our values and expect that people will continue to follow, but we can be agile in other areas, moving and changing to meet demands and increase our capacity for relationship, trust, and positive outcomes.

In a small way, that happened for both of my children today because I "accepted."

Your Leadership Story

What are your "non-negotiables" as a leader?

In situations that fall outside these lines, how willing are you to adjust to accommodate the desires of your constituents?

33 Reflections on My First Race

I finished my first race–a 5k this past Saturday.

I finished the 3.1 miles in 27:43–a pace of 8:56 per mile. I'm fairly pleased with the outcome for two main reasons: first, I had to overcome circumstances because I'd had a cold for most of the previous week, and hadn't run in the 10 days prior to the event. It felt like someone was standing on my chest for most of the race. Second, my goal was to run my first 5k in 9 minute miles, which I accomplished in spite of not feeling 100%.

More importantly, though, it gave me an opportunity to reflect on a few things:

When we realize a goal or milestone in our lives, whether that is a leadership goal or not, we can (and should) realize the people surrounding it. Who helped us make it happen? Who supported us?

In my case, my wife and kids (especially my daughter) have been frequent companions, riding their bikes while I am running. My mom and stepdad joined them for race day also.

The reactions of my children, though, were telling. It was enough that they made "You're my hero" cards, but my daughter ran up to me while I was in the starting throng to give me a hug and kiss and say, "I love you," and my son wore my warm-up top while I raced, and had a bottle of water for me at the finish literally before I could remove the chip timer from my ankle. While I was walking after the race to cool down, he walked beside me with his arm on my back, just like I often do to him.

I also learned something about momentum, and where it comes from. My family is my inspiration for running, mostly because I want to be around as long as possible to see and share their lives. That thought kept me going when I couldn't breathe, and gets me outside when I don't feel like training. It pushes me, also, to run farther, and faster, to inspire them.

For maybe that is what I have learned above all: there is nothing I'd rather be more than someone else's hero.

Your Leadership Story

Who are your primary supporters?

From what sources do you gather momentum?

34 You Have No Idea...

I have an old friend who is involved in an endeavor I consider very noble and worthwhile. Recently, I was able to lend him some support in this.

Almost immediately after, he sent me an email to say thank you that contained a surprising line: "You have no idea the encouragement that it is..."

He was right. I had no idea.

And how often does it happen to us as leaders, whether we hear about it or not, that some action, or encouragement, or decision has a positive effect, perhaps even one we did not intend, but got anyway?

Again I am reminded to be intentional with my impact, careful in its use, and generous in its outpouring.

Your Leadership Story

In what ways could you be more aware of the effect your support has on others?

In what ways could you be more generous with that support?

35 Leading from the Front

My children learned how to ride 2 wheel bicycles this summer, just in time for the start of the school year.

This has been a major boon to our family, as we enjoy being outside, and it solved a pressing problem for us, because the school's bus service does not extend to our area as we are less than a mile from the school.

My wife often leads the bike-to-school trips, and I join when I am able. When we go together, one of us leads, and the other plays caboose.

Recently, we were headed to school together, and my daughter, who rides a bit better than my son, went out ahead with my wife, while I remained behind with my son.

We cross one busy street on our way, which my wife and daughter managed before we reached the intersection. We must negotiate a slight downhill as we approach this street, and so we have to be careful to coast and brake well before arriving.

My son was in front because of the break in our procession, and I called ahead to him to slow down.

He didn't.

I called again.

Still no slow down.

Then, whoosh! Across the intersection he went without braking, and without looking.

He made it, but was lucky to have done so.

I was caught on the other side of the street, but I could see the fear in his face; he knew exactly what had happened.

"Stay there," I said. "I'll be there in a moment."

When I got across, I knew it wasn't the time to chide him for his mistake. I made sure he was OK, told him it was fine with me if his bike went across the street without him if need be in order for him to be safe, and then I established a new plan: "From now on, Dad rides in front."

Riding in front as a leader ensures direction, arguably the most important aspect of leadership. It also enables leading by example, not just directive. When I ride behind my son, I have to tell him to stop, or that it is OK to cross. He might not hear me. He might even ignore what I am telling him. When I am in front, however, he just sees and follows–he knows exactly where we are going and what we are doing. Further, he learns cues for himself, instead of relying on my commands for every decision.

Not to mention, leading from the front is easier in that it causes less stress–it's harder to see in the back, and relationships are better when you are not yelling all the time.

I've thought of it several times since: make sure you are riding in front, Dad.

Your Leadership Story

How have you invited accountability to lead by example, not directive?

If you realize you are leading from the back in certain areas, how can you return to the front and provide direction?

36 When I Grow Up, I Want to Be...

"When I grow up, I want to be..."

Like many, we have this conversation every so often in our house.

My son has been saying, "A police" for some time now (he doesn't add the "officer" part yet).

The other day, he said something different.

"When I grow up, I'm going to be a dad, and a police."

As I consider his comment now, it is, perhaps, the greatest compliment I've ever received.

You see, he wants to be a dad because he sees something good about that role, something worthwhile, something toward which to aspire.

He sees that in me.

I have, for all my life, wanted to be a dad. I cannot remember a time when that was not true.

But my reasons were very different. I wanted to be what I did not have, become what was not modeled for me.

My son wants to become what he has, what I model for him.

If I accomplish nothing else for all my life, still I have won.

When he does become that to which he aspires, and assumes the privilege of fatherhood in better ways than I have, then the goal of my leadership will be achieved.

In the meantime, if I have anything to say about it, he will have many more reasons to want to be "a dad" when he grows up.

On that you could bet your very life.

Your Leadership Story

If you could narrow the purpose of your leadership to one outcome, what would it be?

Have you ever been single minded in your pursuit of a mission? What are you prepared to sacrifice to see it achieved?

37 I Just Want...

My daughter will be 8 in a few weeks. She is growing more confident, more independent.

You wouldn't know it lately, though.

I ran fairly early last Sunday, and it was raining quite hard. We were in the midst of several straight days of rain, and many problems with flooding plagued the area. My daughter was awake when I left, already dressed for church, and wanted to go with me. I told her she had to stay home because of the conditions, at which she began to cry. I nearly relented (something about a daughter's tears...) but went on alone.

A day or two later at bedtime she asked me, "What is your favorite color of the day (I often change my mind about these kinds of things)?"

"Green," I replied.

Five minutes later when I came in to her room to say goodnight, she had her clothes for the next day laid out on her floor—jeans and a green top.

I made sure to compliment her on her appearance the next morning.

After all, what she was (and is) saying in each of these episodes is, "I just want to be with you; I just want you to notice me; I just want your approval; I just want to do what you are doing."

Why?

Because I am her leader.

Your Leadership Story

What consideration have you given to what you are willing to reveal about yourself as a leader, or do with your followers? Do you draw a social line with them?

How do you cultivate attributes that make your followers desire your countenance and your approval?

38 A Simple Thanks

My daughter is a child who likes to arrange things, organize things, and have a plan. This includes her clothing. She often knows what she is going to wear ahead of time, and matches her clothes very well, and very intentionally. She gets up in the morning, cares for herself and her needs, and is ready to go to school on time.

My son, not so much.

So on a recent morning in which my son was having periodic trouble getting himself ready, I did the counterintuitive thing: I left him alone to his devices, and called my daughter to the top of the stairs where I was.

When she arrived, I gave her a big hug, told her she looked lovely, and thanked her for her continued cooperation and independence in getting ready.

She just smiled and went down the stairs.

A simple idea here, and one you've heard before, but is worth repeating: How much time do you spend coaching and correcting non-performers, and how much time do you spend affirming and investing in those followers who are doing exactly what they should be doing?

This time, for me, that ratio was right on.

Your Leadership Story

What percentage of positive behavior in your sphere of influence goes unnoticed or taken for granted?

How could you actively reduce that percentage?

39 A Real Mess

My son made a mess. Not just a "I-spilled-something-and-now-it-has-to-be-cleaned-up-by-an-adult" type of mess, but a mess that started in the hallway, went up the stairs, down another hall, and on to the bathroom floor before it could be contained in the tub.

I'll spare you further details, but it wasn't pretty.

To make matters worse, my only command to him, "Be still," went almost totally unheeded, exacerbating the situation and wearing my patience.

I complained. To him about the mess, about the way he handled it, about the fact that I was the one cleaning it all up...

As I went on, he apologized probably 3 times. Each time arrested my frustration, but only temporarily, as he seemed to have a knack during this particular episode for failing to listen, and somehow, improbably, actually making things worse.

So I'm cleaning, and fuming both inside and out, and he says, "What's the biggest thing you've ever seen?"

"I don't know," I answered. "The Sears Tower, I guess, or the ocean."

"The biggest thing I've ever seen is this mess," he said.

Then it hit me.

This wasn't the biggest thing he'd ever seen, not even

close, but I certainly was acting like it was quite colossal.

"No, it isn't, bud," I told him. "This is not the biggest thing you've ever seen."

Perspective. I'd lost it completely. How often does that happen to us as leaders, though, and how easy it is to lose perspective with those people and situations closest to us, when we never would in other circumstances.

The great irony? I'm normally good in a crisis–I see things more clearly, logically, in an almost detached state of mind. But not this time.

A strikeout (this time) for Dad, but a great leadership lesson.

Your Leadership Story

What message does your level of reaction send to your people?

What safeguards do you employ to ensure you maintain perspective when crisis threatens your composure?

40 When It Rains, Go Outside!

I don't like running–never have. I do it only because I know it is good for me. Sure, when I run I feel better throughout the day, but that usually isn't enough to put me over the hump of disdain for the activity itself.

When it came time to run today, you can imagine my chagrin when I peered out the window to see that it was raining. It wasn't pouring, just raining–a kind of steady, persistent rain that seemed to say, "I might not ruin your day, but I'm going to affect it."

I had an enemy.

Now I'm not a very good starter, but I'm a great finisher. My friend Dave keeps telling me that I need to run races or do something that is going to motivate me to run. He's right, but it isn't because I'm competitive, it's because I like to finish things, and I like to see if I can improve no matter what I'm doing.

I looked outside again, through the rain, and I saw the tree in my mind. The tree that had marked my halfway point on my previous two timed runs–I was going to run past it today in the same amount of time, I decided. In spite of the rain, I was going to improve.

So out into the rain I went. I found a favorite song for inspiration, pressed play on my iPod, and 50 yards into my run, my enemy became my friend. I put my arms out, trying to feel as much of the rain as I could. I breathed in the damp air; I looked up into the rain, and for the first time in a very long while, I enjoyed running.

It was the subtle reframing that got me there. It was the decision that despite the circumstances, I was going to improve. It was thinking about writing this as I was running; it was learning about leadership by making a circumstance irrelevant.

One of my favorite leadership quotations is attributed to Napoleon Bonaparte: "Circumstances? What are circumstances? I make circumstances."

I made circumstances today, and I will use it as a blueprint to do so again.

Your Leadership Story

What circumstances do you need to make irrelevant to further your leadership, a goal you are trying to achieve, or a relationship you want to build?

Consider the last time you overcame an obstacle or made a positive choice. What effect did it have on you?

41 "I'm Sorry."

"I'm sorry."

A good friend and sometimes mentor of mine told me once that the first lesson we must learn as leaders is how to say we're sorry.

This concept is ever so simple to understand, and ever so difficult to practice, much less master.

Tonight after I put my kids to bed, I returned to their rooms after a few minutes to apologize to them.

It was difficult. They'd been disobedient and disrespectful for most of the previous hour. My apology did not change that, nor did it let them off the hook for their behavior. As a matter of fact, I didn't really even want to apologize to them yet because I remained unhappy about the way they had behaved.

However, the way I responded to that behavior in the moment was intimidating—maybe even scary. I did not yell or raise a hand to them, but I know what I look like when I am upset because I have been told, and have seen for myself (it sounds silly, but have you ever stood in front of a mirror to make the faces and gestures you make at others? It is a telling experience, I can assure you.) I know that when I am upset I talk and move more quickly. And I need to be aware of how that affects people, especially people who are very young.

So I apologized to my children, told them that I did not mean to be harsh with them or scare them in any way, and that I am on their side. My son's reassurance was immediate, "I know, you are my dad," he smiled. My daughter did not speak, but her arms around my neck a few moments later gave me all the assurance I needed.

After that, I apologized to my wife for the episode.

Why?

Because I knew it would affect her.

As a leader, I have to discern and interpret the entire situation, for all the stakeholders, not just the ones who are readily apparent.

If I fail to do that, I might only be leading half of my people, but in discerning fully, I ensure that everyone arrives, and arrives together.

Your Leadership Story

What response have you sought about how your actions, especially when you are angry, affect others?

How can you be certain you are observing an entire situation and its effects, not just a partial one?

42 The Better I Know Myself...

...the more equipped I am to lead.

But that can get ugly sometimes.

A story I tell often when I lead workshops and seminars recounts an episode of gaining self-awareness that I will not likely forget. Some time ago, my wife and I were having a conversation about how we communicate and talking about what we do well, and what had changed over time in our marriage, when she said something that took me completely by surprise: "When we have a conflict or disagreement, you sometimes intimidate me."

"WHAT?!"

I was flabbergasted. We'd been married for 7 or 8 years at that point. My first thought was, "How could I not know something like that?" and my second was, "Great, I've been intimidating my wife every time we have a disagreement for all this time and have lacked the sensitivity to realize it until told. I'm doing something really wrong here."

I apologized, and suggested that we have some kind of mechanism by which she could "call time out" if that ever happened again. "I would never intimidate you on purpose," I assured her. "I would readily admit to intimidating someone else on purpose; in fact, I'd certainly intimidate someone else on your behalf, but I would never knowingly do that to you."

"I know," she said, "the fact that you are that way on my behalf is something I really appreciate about you, and I know you aren't that way with me on purpose, so I just remind myself of that..." (Did I mention how gracious and kind my wife is?)

You see, it is certainly part of who I am on occasion to be intimidating or terse, whether I intend to be or not. Sometimes that results in something very positive, and sometimes, unfortunately, it does not.

So it follows that my personality is not best applied by letting other people make of it what they will–especially because some of the people about whom I care most and desire most to lead cannot so easily discern my intent.

Imagine being 6 or 7 years old and having a "direct" dad–it could be hard to make sense of that from time to time, wouldn't it? And you might be scared or confused, but not have the means or proper words to express that.

No, I simply cannot afford to "be myself" and let things happen as they will. I must know myself well enough to manage who I am so that I can lead well. Moreover, I need to know those I lead to discern the path that enables who I am and how I lead to create the greatest good for everyone involved.

Your Leadership Story

Are you wielding your personality, or is your personality wielding you?

What are some of the unintended consequences you have experienced from "just being you?"

43 Saying 'Yes' and Letting Go

Today was a beautiful day in Chicagoland–nearly perfect–
70 degrees, light breeze, sunny... the kind of day we
experience in this area only a handful of times each spring,
and then another handful in the autumn.

For my part, I spent virtually the entire day inside, packing
for our upcoming move.

My son, though, wanted no part of these adult chores, and
just after lunch, he said to me, "Dad, I'm going outside to
ride my scooter, OK?"

"Sure," I said.

"I'll only go up and down the driveway," he replied,
anticipating my next comment.

My children are reaching the ages at which they desire
greater independence–freedom to try new things, to
venture a bit further from home, and to see what there is to
see "out there."

All parents know that this stage of development is difficult–
both for the child and for the adult–and it is ever important
to lead in these situations.

As I thought about my son's simple request, I was glad for
having said yes. I say no often enough, and it occurs to
me that leading ought to be more about saying yes than it
is about saying no as a general rule. The reason, simply,
is that yes leads to possibility, and no eliminates it. I could
have ruined a perfect day for my son with one word. I'm
glad I chose not to.

Your Leadership Story

What opportunity did you create the last time you said yes?

When was the last time you were uncomfortable after having given permission to a follower? How did it turn out?

44 "I know."

I tell my kids "I love you" every day.

A couple of days ago, however, I was confronted with an unusual response from my son: "I know." At first I was a bit taken aback, but I resisted my first inclination, which was to say, "You are supposed to reply, 'I love you too.'" Instead, I took it as a compliment.

Why?

Because in that moment, I knew my love for my son had become predictable to him. He counts on it, accepts it, understands it, and knows how I will respond to things based on my love for him.

One of the litmus tests I use with leaders is what I call "The Predictability Factor." I ask them: "If I was to take all of your direct reports, and present them with a real-life scenario with which they would be familiar, then ask them, 'How would (Leader) respond to this?' how quickly would they reach consensus?"

Most leaders don't know, or overestimate their predictability, necessitating work on their performance in this critical area.

My son thinks I'm predictable in one of the areas that matters most, which is an occasion for celebration, but also for continued attention.

Your Leadership Story

How well are you landing your critical messages with your constituents?

Once landed, how do you make those messages permanent?

45 Hey Pioneer!

Virtually everyone agrees that vision is an essential component of leadership. Call it forward looking, inspirational or vivid–the message is the same. Leaders must concern themselves with what is next.

To accomplish this, leaders must scout the territory. When pioneers were exploring this country, they had scouts, parties who would go before the rest of the convoy to determine the best way forward and forecast danger when it lay ahead.

That, however, was not the most essential part. The absolutely indispensable action was circling back to inform and brief the rest of the party before riding on again.

Failing to "circle back" causes many leaders to fail.

My wife and I recently agreed terms for the purchase of a home. It is, of course, an exciting time, but it is fraught with uncertainty, and promises certain difficulty. I've decided it is not unlike pioneering in many ways.

In our family, I am the scout. I tend to see further into the future than my wife does, and I am also much more inclined to enjoy change (even change for change's sake). And therein lies the leadership problem: if I fail to "circle back" to reassure her that we are making the right decision financially, socially and geographically, she will begin to lose heart, and will rightly conclude that I am not supporting her adequately.

Imagine what it would have been like for those in a pioneering convoy if they had not heard from their scouts for an extended period. Surely they would begin to wonder if something catastrophic had occurred. They would also begin to doubt their prospects for the future, and that is the first step toward losing hope.

Wherever we are leading, our role as leaders is to scout the territory, and then, more importantly, communicate what we have seen effectively.

But it doesn't end there...

It doesn't end there because it isn't enough to "circle back" just to inform everyone else what we, as leaders, have decided to do based on what we have seen up ahead.

Instead, we must inform, and then solicit input. To continue with the analogy I used earlier, if I scout the territory ahead, and then simply inform my wife, "We're moving," I am making a terrific mistake. But even leaders who do the "circling back" part well often fail at this second step.

Leadership is not a brain trust. It is not huddling in a secret room somewhere, or on a private retreat, dreaming up ways to "cast our vision" or create "mission statements" to plaster on every wall available.

When I coach leaders who talk about their visions or their mission statements, I often ask them, "How many people contributed to that?" If the answer is a handful or fewer, I know we have some work to do together.

Back to my previous example regarding the purchase of a new house: my children are very young. When I "circle back" to them (this must be done both individually and collectively–another point at which leaders fail), I certainly do not expect them to decide where we will live. However, I do have to be very careful that once some of the decisions that only their mother and I can make are made, we provide them with some autonomy and influence on other things. For example, my wife has initiated the idea that we will let them choose from among several options for the decor of their rooms. This way, they have some ownership in the direction we take together in furnishing and creating our home. Incidentally, this idea never would have surfaced if I had not "circled back" to my wife, and then heard her input in earnest. It is a great idea, and I cannot take credit for it, because I would not have thought of it without her. It has improved my thinking about our move, though, and therefore my leadership.

Just this morning as we walked to the bus stop, my daughter commented on the beauty of a neighbor's flowerbed.

"Would you like to have flowers at our new house?" I asked her.

"Yes," she replied.

"Then you can help us pick them, and then help us plant them. Would you like that?"

"Um hmm, I can dig the holes," she responded.

"Absolutely," I replied, "and you can put the plants in, too."

It is especially important for our family to engage my daughter in this process, and to find ways in which she can own, and enjoy, this move. She is more embedded in her school activities and friends than my son is, and has expressed hesitation and sorrow about leaving them. Giving her these experiences will soothe those fears, in part, and help her to accept our new area as desirable because she did something to make it that way.

The difficult work is not circling back, it is suspending judgment for long enough to ensure that the voices of our constituents are heard, and then ensuring that our path takes a direction informed by their input.

Your Leadership Story

Do you circle back at regular intervals to reassure and gather opinions? How often?

In what ways can you give your followers greater autonomy to establish direction with you as their leader?

46 "You Didn't Even Notice Me!"

A couple of days ago I woke up, came upstairs and saw my son on the couch watching television. I walked up to him, put my hand on his head and greeted him with a hearty, "Good morning."

After that, I walked down the hallway, and just as I was turning, my daughter came out of her room. No sooner had I walked past her than she turned and said, "You didn't even notice me!"

OUCH!

She was right—I had failed to greet her in the same way I'd greeted her brother. I had embarked upon on a mission to do something else, and wasn't looking for her, or for other opportunities besides the one on which I'd already decided.

I turned to her and gave her a big hug. She smiled up at me and I kidded with her, saying, "You must have sneaked past me."

She understood, but I'll have to be careful next time.

Your Leadership Story

What have you been on a mission to do, to the neglect of other, perhaps more important, things?

As a leader, what are you doing that might be perceived as favoritism or unfair?

47 Is the L-E-A-D-E-R around?

A few days ago my children spent the day with a family friend, and something unusual happened. My friend was babysitting a little girl, perhaps 2 years of age, who came into the room just as we arrived. Within a few seconds, she was standing at my feet, looking up at me with her arms extended for me to pick her up.

Now, I am not the most approachable person in the world. I've been told in my life that I am unapproachable, intense, even intimidating. I tend to keep my own counsel about things, and find myself an observer, not a participant, in most situations unless I am there to lead or facilitate. It is still cold here in Chicago, and I have not yet resolved to shave off my winter's beard, and have also let my hair grow long. All of this to say that although I am ever so fond of children, they usually don't seek me out for companionship, so this little girl's insistence was quite out of the ordinary.

I picked her up, and she immediately leaned her head on my shoulder. As I continued talking to my friend, she said of the little girl, "She does the same thing to my husband; her D-A-D-D-Y isn't around any more, so..."

When I returned to pick up my children, the little girl had just awakened from a nap–she no sooner was taken out of the crib and set on the ground than she walked directly to me with the same appeal to be picked up. I obliged as I had in the morning, which elicited a similar reaction from her.

It occurred to me with some sadness as I left that this little girl knew exactly what she was looking for: someone strong, someone safe, someone she could trust. She was, in some small way, looking to fill a void she knew she had, though in some ways could not possibly express.

So it is with us, and with our constituents. Each of us looks for something from our leaders, sometimes a thing just beyond our ability to describe, but we are looking nonetheless. Whether we are leading in the home or elsewhere, it is our role, in part, to discover that for which our constituents are searching, and provide it for them. In this small example, I was able to provide, if ever so briefly, what my little friend was seeking. I knew exactly what she wanted, even if she didn't, and far be it from me to withhold it from her when it was mine to give.

Your Leadership Story

Who in your life and sphere of influence is wondering if the L-E-A-D-E-R is around?

What have you done to ensure they find you?

48 Trust Enables

My family and I just returned from a long weekend in Wisconsin. It was a nice time, but the phenomenon of road travel lingers with me as much as the event now that I am home.

You see, an interesting thing happens in my family when we take a long car ride together–certainly you have experienced it too: people who are not driving fall asleep. As we traveled home yesterday, I had a moment to contemplate this as I was moving at 5 miles per hour through a traffic jam. It occurred to me in that moment that my family falling asleep is as much about my leadership as it is about their fatigue from the weekend's events.

They trust me.

They know that when they wake up, we will be closer to home–our desired destination–than when we started. We won't have veered off course accidentally, or changed directions to head somewhere else without their knowledge or consent. In fact, it is unlikely that we will even have altered the course we set out for ourselves ahead of time.

They trust me because they have had a voice in the plan. They want to go home, and they know I can get them there. They are free to pursue more than just sleep as a result of this knowledge–they can watch a movie, eat, play games, or talk. Everything they do on the trip comes from trusting that the destination has not changed, and that I, as the leader of our family, am the most qualified person to get them where they want to go.

Imagine the scene if this trust didn't exist: 2 back seat

drivers and 2 front seat drivers, debating the merits of each prospective route, and discontent with their respective roles...

But none of this happens because of trust. I have capital with them; they'll even forgive me if I make a mistake and get us lost temporarily (which happens sometimes). They'll give me the flexibility to take a different route if we run into traffic; change the plan if bad weather arises and we need to stop for a while (which also happens sometimes).

It is easy, of course, to accomplish this for a 3 hour car ride. However, the principle for leading in other situations follows a similar formula.

Trust enables your destination, your people and your leadership.

Your Leadership Story

Do you have trust capital with your constituents? What have you done to establish it?

Have you communicated the destination and involved them in the process of planning?

49 What Is Your Goal?

Sitting at the dinner table tonight as a family, we were debriefing our day when my son revealed that his "goal" at school is "not to worry about what other people are doing."

"Is that your goal, or did someone else give it to you?" I asked, knowing the forthcoming answer.

"My teacher gave it to me," came the predictable response.

"Are you the only one who has a goal, or do all of your classmates have one too?"

"Everyone."

"So what are some of the other goals?" I continued.

"Well, Jeremy's is not to talk so much, and Jack's is to eat all of his lunch and not make mad faces at his food, and…"

"I see. Well, I'm going to change your goal," I declared. My son looked at me like what I was suggesting was not possible. "I'm changing your goal," I continued, "because I don't like it. It is framed negatively, and it isn't a good goal. What if, instead of making your goal not to worry about what other people are doing, we change it into ensuring that you help someone every day?" I offered.

"I do that; I help my friends," he responded.

"Great, and that is a very good thing to do. This way, you can make sure that when you are thinking about what other people are doing, it is so that you can help them," I posited.

"OK," he agreed.

"Why are you looking at me like that?" I said to my wife.

"Because I have a feeling you are going to be having a conversation with his teacher soon," she replied with a knowing look.

Perhaps, but what is important here is that real goals are not assigned, they are chosen. My son helps people, and therefore sometimes fails to mind his own business, because he wants to be involved in their lives. No measure of intervention will change that. It is my job as his father, and our job as leaders, to assist people to be more of who they are, not less. Sometimes, of course, this requires some reframing, or redirection, but our interventions must be motivated by helping them to define their own goals, measure whether or not they have achieved them, and ensure that alignment exists between the goal and the identity of the person.

Sometimes this requires permission to challenge an assumption; to push back or break a rule. My son has this permission now. How he uses it will be up to him, but I've empowered him to handle it in the way he sees fit, knowing that I will support him whatever he chooses to do.

It won't surprise me if I don't have to make the call to that teacher...

Your Leadership Story

How do you arrive at goals for your people? Prescription? Solicitation? Agreement?

In what circumstances do you find it acceptable to break the rules and empower others to do the same?

50 Legacy

Legacy has 2 directions: past and future. Most of the time when we consider this concept, we think about it from the perspective of what our legacy will be–the future perspective. Both are worth considering, though.

All of us are products of someone else's legacy. In fact, we are likely products of the legacy of multiple people.

Our primary influencers in life–those whose legacies have the first chance to shape us–are our parents. My mother's legacy to me has been one of industry and self-reliance. My father's legacy, however, was most unfortunate. I did not have the privilege of knowing his greater qualities; growing up I knew only that he could not break the hold of a terrible addiction on his life, and that his life ended prematurely–by his own hand.

As a result, I have lived much of my life motivated by moving away from that legacy, instead of toward another.

Stephen Covey would call me a transition person. I am the first of my line; that is my legacy. My children, and their children, will never know the pain that I have known. It is the one area in which I am totally confident that I lead well.

Our legacies as leaders can be measured by the influence we wield when we are not present. To enjoy a true legacy as leaders, things must become demonstrably better after we are gone because of our enabling while we were present. I say demonstrably on purpose, for if it falls apart after we've left it, we weren't really leading. But if it thrives because of our efforts while we were present, that is leading indeed.

Your Leadership Story

How will you measure your legacy both qualitatively and quantitatively?

What gives you confidence that you are leading well so that future generations of leaders will benefit from your influence?

Notes

Notes

Notes

Notes

Notes

Notes

Notes

About the Author

Stosh D. Walsh serves others as a coach, consultant and speaker throughout North America and Europe. His past clients include Microsoft, Hewlett-Packard, Ann Inc., US Bank, McKinsey and Company, Banana Republic, Northrop Grumman, Kohler and the United States Federal Government. He has an undergraduate degree in Education and a Master's degree in Leadership. Stosh's outside interests include photography and hiking. He lives in Chicago's western suburbs with his wife, Tammy, and their two children. This is his first book.

Stosh welcomes the opportunity to interact with readers via the following outlets:
Twitter: @stoshdwalsh
Facebook: Stosh D. Walsh - Writer
email: stoshdwalsh@gmail.com

About 2nd Place Press

2nd Place Press exists to provide enrichment materials for leaders at all levels. Its mission is to accelerate the journey of others through print media, offering practical insights for application in both organizational and personal settings.